Makers as INNOVATORS JUNIOR

Making Slime

By Amy Quinn

CHERRY LAKE
Publishing

Published in the United States of America by
Cherry Lake Publishing
Ann Arbor, Michigan
www.cherrylakepublishing.com

Series Editor: Kristin Fontichiaro
Reading Adviser: Marla Conn, MD, Ed., Literacy Specialist,
Read-Ability, Inc.
Photo Credits: All photos by Amy Quinn

Library of Congress Cataloging-in-Publication Data
Names: Quinn, Amy, 1976- author.
Title: Making slime / by Amy Quinn.
Description: Ann Arbor, Michigan : Cherry Lake Publishing, [2018] | Series: Makers as
  innovators junior | Series: 21st century skills innovation library | Includes bibliographical
  references and index.
Identifiers: LCCN 2017032489 | ISBN 9781534107830 (lib. bdg.) | ISBN 9781534109810
  (pdf) | ISBN 9781534108820 (pbk.) | ISBN 9781534120808 (ebook)
Subjects: LCSH: Gums and resins, Synthetic—Juvenile literature.
Classification: LCC TP978 .Q56 2018 | DDC 620.1/924—dc23
  LC record available at https://lccn.loc.gov/2017032489

Cherry Lake Publishing would like to acknowledge the work of The Partnership for
21st Century Learning. Please visit *www.p21.org* for more information.

Printed in the United States of America
Corporate Graphics

A Note to Adults: Please review the instructions for the activities in this book before allowing children to do them. Be sure to help them with any activities you do not think they can safely comple' ~~ their own.

A Note to Kids: Be sure to ask an adult for help with these activities when you need it. Always put your safety first!

Table of Contents

Slime is so much fun to stretch and pull!

Mix It Up!

Do you enjoy mixing things together? Do you like using your science skills to create new things? Then let's try making something new: slime! Slime is a lot of fun to make and play with. Keep reading to find out how to make your own gooey slime!

Keep It Clean

Make sure you have adult permission before doing science experiments such as making slime. Put newspaper or a vinyl tablecloth on the table to help clean up any spills. Make sure to wash your hands after you make or play with slime.

Gather all the supplies you'll need before you start mixing your slime.

What You'll Need

- 7 ounces of white or clear glue
- Bowl and wooden stick
- 2 tablespoons of water
- 1 tablespoon of acrylic paint
- 1 teaspoon of baking soda
- 2 tablespoons of contact lens solution

Making Changes

Make slime using the recipe above first. Then try making it with **substitutions**. You could use food coloring instead of acrylic paint. Instead of contact solution, you could mix 1 teaspoon of Borax powder with 1 cup of warm water. It is fun to experiment and see what combination you like best!

It is fun to watch how each ingredient changes the slime as you mix it.

Basic Slime Recipe

Follow these steps to make perfect slime!

1. Pour the glue into the bowl.
2. Mix the water with the glue. Use the wooden stick to stir.
3. Add the acrylic paint and stir.
4. Slowly mix in the baking soda.
5. Add the contact solution a little bit at a time. Stir 10 times. Add more contact solution if the mixture is too sticky.

Pick up your slime with your hands. Rub it back and forth. Make sure you like the **consistency**!

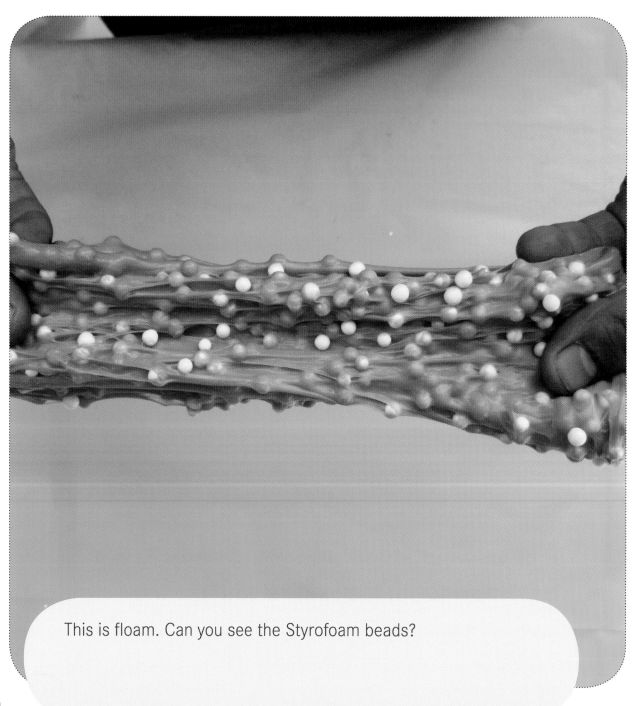

This is floam. Can you see the Styrofoam beads?

Fluffy Slime and Floam

Would you like to add fluffiness or **texture** to your slime? To make fluffy slime, add a squirt of shaving cream. Mix it into your basic slime recipe before you add the water. This will also make your slime smell great!

Mix Styrofoam beads into the slime to create floam. Floam makes it easy to form slime into shapes. It feels bumpy and extra squishy! This is texture!

Science is happening here. When you mix the ingredients, you create a chemical change.

The Science of Slime

Most slime has two important ingredients. It needs a **polymer** (found in glue) and a **borate ion** (found in contact solution). These give the slime its consistency. Mixing these two things together creates a change. The result acts like a liquid and a solid at the same time! It becomes the thick, gooey slime we love!

You can dress up your slime with stuff you have around the house.

Slime Bar

Want to organize the things you add to your slime? Create a slime bar! Look around your house for leftover art supplies. Then set out bowls with these supplies on a table. Glitter will make slime sparkle. Beads will change its texture. Sequins, gems, foam pieces, or small plastic toys can also be added. Putting small things in your slime makes it more fun and creative. Make your slime unusual!

Slime feels like a liquid. Yet it holds its shape when you pull it.

Playing with Slime

The fun part is playing with your slime! You can pull it apart and stretch it out. Try poking your fingers in it to make a popping sound. Roll your slime into balls or long snakes. Press together two different colored slimes to create a colorful twist. Use your hands to push, pull, and squish the slime.

You can name your slime. Make extra to share with friends!

Organizing and Storing Slime

Store your slime in a sealed **container**. You can use small jars or plastic bags. A clear jar makes it easy to see what color slime is inside. Don't forget to label it. Make sure to play with your slime every day. If it dries out, just throw it away. Then start over again!

Helpful Hints

It is easiest to make slime in small batches. Then you can tell if you need to add anything. It might need more glue or color. The more you stir, the better it will turn out. Before you know it, you will become a slime expert!

You can decorate your slime however you want!

Naming and Trading

Be creative with your slime play. Give your slime a silly name. Or give it a purpose. If it's banana yellow, it could be food for monkeys. Or maybe it could be unicorn food. Use your imagination! Do you need more items for your slime bar? Trading these items and even slime can give you more choices. Invite your friends over and share ideas.

Working Together

Think of something you could make with friends. Try building a slime ocean, a slime city, or a slime park. Make slime colors to match holidays or celebrations. Show off your slime by making videos of your creations!

Glossary

borate ion (BOR-ate EYE-ahn) one of the two substances needed to make slime; it is found in contact solution

consistency (kuhn-SIS-tuhn-see) the way in which a substance holds together

container (kuhn-TAY-nur) an object used to hold something

polymer (PAH-luh-mur) one of the two substances needed to make slime; it is found in glue

substitutions (sub-stuh-TOO-shuhnz) things used in place of other things

texture (TEKS-chur) how something feels

Find Out More

Books

Gregory, Josh. *Junior Scientists: Experiment with Solids.* Ann Arbor, MI: Cherry Lake Publishing, 2011.

Simon, Charnan. *Compounds and Mixtures.* Ann Arbor, MI: Cherry Lake Publishing, 2010.

Web Sites

Kids Activities Blog
http://kidsactivitiesblog.com
Check out some easy ideas for arts and crafts projects.

Science Bob
https://sciencebob.com
This site has a lot of fun science experiments you can try.

Index

About the Author

Amy Quinn is a first-grade teacher in West Bloomfield, Michigan. She is also a coach and mentor for FIRST LEGO League (FLL) and a team manager for Destination Imagination. Amy has a daughter, Emily, and a son, Tommy, who both love to design and create new things!